the
book
of
good

a journal to help you
find the good in each day

Sometimes it can be hard to find the good in each day. But it's out there—you just have to teach yourself how to find it.

This journal is for those looking for a way to stop negativity from dominating your thoughts. All you have to do is write three good things that happened each day—no matter how small or inconsequential they feel.

Each day, write three good things, and after a few weeks, it'll start to get easier. Will it turn the world into rainbows and puppies?

No.

But isn't it worth trying?

THE BOOK OF GOOD: NATURE

Published by Left-Handed Mitten Publications
ISBN-13: 978-1706263029
UPC

Writing, book design, and formatting by Melanie Hooyenga.
Website: melaniehoo.com
Email: melaniehooyenga@gmail.com
Newsletter: melaniehoo.com/hoos-letter
Twitter & Instagram: @melaniehoo
Facebook: MelanieHooyenga
PO Box 554, Grand Haven, MI 49417

Cover design by Adrienne Whisman.
Website: awanderingnomad.com

the
book
of
good

Left-Handed Mitten
Publications

This journal belongs to

week 1 ....

Sunday ....

....

....

Monday ....

....

....

Tuesday ....

....

....

Wednesday ....

....

....

Thursday _____

_____

_____

Friday _____

_____

_____

Saturday _____

_____

_____

Three best things this week

_____

_____

_____

week 2 _____

Sunday _____

_____

_____

Monday _____

_____

_____

Tuesday _____

_____

_____

Wednesday _____

_____

_____

Thursday _____

_____

_____

Friday _____

_____

_____

Saturday _____

_____

_____

Three best things this week

_____

_____

_____

week 3 _____

Sunday _____

_____

_____

Monday _____

_____

_____

Tuesday _____

_____

_____

Wednesday _____

_____

_____

Thursday

Friday

Saturday

Three best things this week

week 4 _____

Sunday _____

_____

_____

Monday _____

_____

_____

Tuesday _____

_____

_____

Wednesday _____

_____

_____

Thursday _____

_____

_____

Friday _____

_____

_____

Saturday _____

_____

_____

Three best things this week

_____

_____

_____

week 5 _____

Sunday _____

_____

_____

Monday _____

_____

_____

Tuesday _____

_____

_____

Wednesday _____

_____

_____

Thursday _____

_____

_____

Friday _____

_____

_____

Saturday _____

_____

_____

Three best things this week

_____

_____

_____

week 6 _____

Sunday _____

_____

_____

Monday _____

_____

_____

Tuesday _____

_____

_____

Wednesday _____

_____

_____

Thursday _____

_____

_____

Friday _____

_____

_____

Saturday _____

_____

_____

Three best things this week

_____

_____

_____

week 7 _____

Sunday _____

_____

_____

Monday _____

_____

_____

Tuesday _____

_____

_____

Wednesday _____

_____

_____

Thursday _____

Friday _____

Saturday _____

Three best things this week

week 8 _____

Sunday _____

Monday _____

Tuesday _____

Wednesday _____

Thursday

Friday

Saturday

Three best things this week

week 9 _____

Sunday _____

_____

_____

Monday _____

_____

_____

Tuesday _____

_____

_____

Wednesday _____

_____

_____

Thursday

Friday

Saturday

Three best things this week

week 10 _____

Sunday _____

_____

_____

Monday _____

_____

_____

Tuesday _____

_____

_____

Wednesday _____

_____

_____

Thursday

Friday

Saturday

Three best things this week

week 11 _____

Sunday _____

_____

_____

Monday _____

_____

_____

Tuesday _____

_____

_____

Wednesday _____

_____

_____

Thursday _____

_____

_____

Friday _____

_____

_____

Saturday _____

_____

_____

Three best things this week

_____

_____

_____

week 12 _____

Sunday _____

_____

_____

Monday _____

_____

_____

Tuesday _____

_____

_____

Wednesday _____

_____

_____

Thursday _____

_____

_____

Friday _____

_____

_____

Saturday _____

_____

_____

Three best things this week

_____

_____

_____

week 13 _____

Sunday _____

_____

_____

Monday _____

_____

_____

Tuesday _____

_____

_____

Wednesday _____

_____

_____

Thursday

Friday

Saturday

Three best things this week

You've made it past the first few months! By now, coming up with three good things should be feeling more natural.

Take a moment to reflect on any changes in your thinking, or your general outlook on the world.

week 14 _____

Sunday _____
_____
_____

Monday _____
_____
_____

Tuesday _____
_____
_____

Wednesday _____
_____
_____

Thursday _____

_____

_____

Friday _____

_____

_____

Saturday _____

_____

_____

Three best things this week

_____

_____

_____

week 15 _____

Sunday _____

_____

_____

Monday _____

_____

_____

Tuesday _____

_____

_____

Wednesday _____

_____

_____

Thursday

Friday

Saturday

Three best things this week

week 16

Sunday

Monday

Tuesday

Wednesday

Thursday _____

_____

_____

Friday _____

_____

_____

Saturday _____

_____

_____

Three best things this week

_____

_____

_____

week 17 _____

Sunday _____

_____

_____

Monday _____

_____

_____

Tuesday _____

_____

_____

Wednesday _____

_____

_____

Thursday _____

_____

_____

Friday _____

_____

_____

Saturday _____

_____

_____

Three best things this week

_____

_____

_____

week 18 _____

Sunday _____

_____

_____

Monday _____

_____

_____

Tuesday _____

_____

_____

Wednesday _____

_____

_____

Thursday _____

_____

_____

Friday _____

_____

_____

Saturday _____

_____

_____

Three best things this week

_____

_____

_____

week 19

Sunday

Monday

Tuesday

Wednesday

Thursday _____

_____

_____

Friday _____

_____

_____

Saturday _____

_____

_____

Three best things this week

_____

_____

_____

week 20 _____

Sunday _____

_____

_____

Monday _____

_____

_____

Tuesday _____

_____

_____

Wednesday _____

_____

_____

Thursday _____

_____

_____

Friday _____

_____

_____

Saturday _____

_____

_____

Three best things this week

_____

_____

_____

week 21 _____

Sunday _____

_____

_____

Monday _____

_____

_____

Tuesday _____

_____

_____

Wednesday _____

_____

_____

Thursday

Friday

Saturday

Three best things this week

week 22 _____

Sunday _____

_____

_____

Monday _____

_____

_____

Tuesday _____

_____

_____

Wednesday _____

_____

_____

Thursday

Friday

Saturday

Three best things this week

week 23 ....

Sunday ....

Monday ....

Tuesday ....

Wednesday ....

Thursday _____

_____

_____

Friday _____

_____

_____

Saturday _____

_____

_____

Three best things this week

_____

_____

_____

week 24 _____

Sunday _____

_____

_____

Monday _____

_____

_____

Tuesday _____

_____

_____

Wednesday _____

_____

_____

Thursday _____

_____

_____

Friday _____

_____

_____

Saturday _____

_____

_____

Three best things this week

_____

_____

_____

week 25 _____

Sunday _____

_____

_____

Monday _____

_____

_____

Tuesday _____

_____

_____

Wednesday _____

_____

_____

Thursday _____

_____

_____

Friday _____

_____

_____

Saturday _____

_____

_____

Three best things this week

_____

_____

_____

week 26 _____

Sunday _____

_____

_____

Monday _____

_____

_____

Tuesday _____

_____

_____

Wednesday _____

_____

_____

Thursday

Friday

Saturday

Three best things this week

You're halfway there! Your three good things should be a habit by now, and you might catch yourself noting good things as they happen so you can write them down later.

Take a moment to reflect on any changes in your thinking, or your general outlook on the world.

week 27 _____

Sunday _____

_____

_____

Monday _____

_____

_____

Tuesday _____

_____

_____

Wednesday _____

_____

_____

Thursday _____

_____

_____

Friday _____

_____

_____

Saturday _____

_____

_____

Three best things this week

_____

_____

_____

week 28 _____

Sunday _____

_____

_____

Monday _____

_____

_____

Tuesday _____

_____

_____

Wednesday _____

_____

_____

Thursday _____

_____

_____

Friday _____

_____

_____

Saturday _____

_____

_____

Three best things this week

_____

_____

_____

week 29 _____

Sunday _____

_____

_____

Monday _____

_____

_____

Tuesday _____

_____

_____

Wednesday _____

_____

_____

Thursday _____

_____

_____

Friday _____

_____

_____

Saturday _____

_____

_____

Three best things this week

_____

_____

_____

week 30 _____

Sunday _____

_____

_____

Monday _____

_____

_____

Tuesday _____

_____

_____

Wednesday _____

_____

_____

Thursday _____

_____

_____

Friday _____

_____

_____

Saturday _____

_____

_____

Three best things this week

_____

_____

_____

week 31 _____

Sunday _____

_____

_____

Monday _____

_____

_____

Tuesday _____

_____

_____

Wednesday _____

_____

_____

Thursday

Friday

Saturday

Three best things this week

Sunday _____

_____

_____

Monday _____

_____

_____

Tuesday _____

_____

_____

Wednesday _____

_____

_____

Thursday _____

_____

_____

Friday _____

_____

_____

Saturday _____

_____

_____

Three best things this week

_____

_____

_____

week 33 _____

Sunday _____

_____

_____

Monday _____

_____

_____

Tuesday _____

_____

_____

Wednesday _____

_____

_____

Thursday

Friday

Saturday

Three best things this week

week 34 _____

Sunday _____

_____

_____

Monday _____

_____

_____

Tuesday _____

_____

_____

Wednesday _____

_____

_____

Thursday _____

_____

_____

Friday _____

_____

_____

Saturday _____

_____

_____

Three best things this week

_____

_____

_____

week 35 _____

Sunday _____

_____

_____

Monday _____

_____

_____

Tuesday _____

_____

_____

Wednesday _____

_____

_____

Thursday _____

_____

_____

Friday _____

_____

_____

Saturday _____

_____

_____

Three best things this week

_____

_____

_____

week 36 _____

Sunday _____

_____

_____

Monday _____

_____

_____

Tuesday _____

_____

_____

Wednesday _____

_____

_____

Thursday _____

_____

_____

Friday _____

_____

_____

Saturday _____

_____

_____

Three best things this week

_____

_____

_____

week 37 _____

Sunday _____

_____

_____

Monday _____

_____

_____

Tuesday _____

_____

_____

Wednesday _____

_____

_____

Thursday _____

_____

_____

Friday _____

_____

_____

Saturday _____

_____

_____

Three best things this week

_____

_____

_____

week 38 _____

Sunday _____

_____

_____

Monday _____

_____

_____

Tuesday _____

_____

_____

Wednesday _____

_____

_____

Thursday _____

_____

_____

Friday _____

_____

_____

Saturday _____

_____

_____

Three best things this week

_____

_____

_____

week 39

Sunday

Monday

Tuesday

Wednesday

Thursday

Friday

Saturday

Three best things this week

Did you ever think you'd make it three-quarters of the year? Writing three good things each day is just part of what you do now, so go ahead and take a moment to reflect on any changes in your thinking, or your general outlook on the world.

week 40 _____

Sunday _____

_____

_____

Monday _____

_____

_____

Tuesday _____

_____

_____

Wednesday _____

_____

_____

Thursday _____

_____

_____

Friday _____

_____

_____

Saturday _____

_____

_____

Three best things this week

_____

_____

_____

week 41 _____

Sunday _____

_____

_____

Monday _____

_____

_____

Tuesday _____

_____

_____

Wednesday _____

_____

_____

Thursday _____

_____

_____

Friday _____

_____

_____

Saturday _____

_____

_____

Three best things this week

_____

_____

_____

week 42 _____

Sunday _____

_____

_____

Monday _____

_____

_____

Tuesday _____

_____

_____

Wednesday _____

_____

_____

Thursday _____

_____

_____

Friday _____

_____

_____

Saturday _____

_____

_____

Three best things this week

_____

_____

_____

week 43 _____

Sunday _____

_____

_____

Monday _____

_____

_____

Tuesday _____

_____

_____

Wednesday _____

_____

_____

Thursday _____

_____

_____

Friday _____

_____

_____

Saturday _____

_____

_____

Three best things this week

_____

_____

_____

week 44 _____

Sunday _____

_____

_____

Monday _____

_____

_____

Tuesday _____

_____

_____

Wednesday _____

_____

_____

Thursday _____

_____

_____

Friday _____

_____

_____

Saturday _____

_____

_____

Three best things this week

_____

_____

_____

week 45 _____

Sunday _____

_____

_____

Monday _____

_____

_____

Tuesday _____

_____

_____

Wednesday _____

_____

_____

Thursday _____

_____

_____

Friday _____

_____

_____

Saturday _____

_____

_____

Three best things this week

_____

_____

_____

week 46 _____

Sunday _____

_____

_____

Monday _____

_____

_____

Tuesday _____

_____

_____

Wednesday _____

_____

_____

Thursday

Friday

Saturday

Three best things this week

week 47 _____

Sunday _____

_____

_____

Monday _____

_____

_____

Tuesday _____

_____

_____

Wednesday _____

_____

_____

Thursday _____

_____

_____

Friday _____

_____

_____

Saturday _____

_____

_____

Three best things this week

_____

_____

_____

week 48 _____

Sunday _____

_____

_____

Monday _____

_____

_____

Tuesday _____

_____

_____

Wednesday _____

_____

_____

Thursday _____

_____

_____

Friday _____

_____

_____

Saturday _____

_____

_____

Three best things this week

_____

_____

_____

week 49 _____

Sunday _____

_____

_____

Monday _____

_____

_____

Tuesday _____

_____

_____

Wednesday _____

_____

_____

Thursday

Friday

Saturday

Three best things this week

week 50 _____

Sunday _____

_____

_____

Monday _____

_____

_____

Tuesday _____

_____

_____

Wednesday _____

_____

_____

Thursday _____

_____

_____

Friday _____

_____

_____

Saturday _____

_____

_____

Three best things this week

_____

_____

_____

week 51 _____

Sunday _____

_____

_____

Monday _____

_____

_____

Tuesday _____

_____

_____

Wednesday _____

_____

_____

Thursday _____

_____

_____

Friday _____

_____

_____

Saturday _____

_____

_____

Three best things this week

_____

_____

_____

week 52 _____

Sunday _____

_____

_____

Monday _____

_____

_____

Tuesday _____

_____

_____

Wednesday _____

_____

_____

Thursday _____

_____

_____

Friday _____

_____

_____

Saturday _____

_____

_____

Three best things this week

_____

_____

_____

Congratulations, you made it!

Hopefully you've reached a point where the good
in each day is no longer elusive. Where hope lingers
longer than despair. Where the world has turned into
rainbow and puppies.

On this last page, take a moment to write down three
things that stood out this year. Something that changed
your outlook, or made you realize that there is good in
the world if you just take a moment to pay attention.

Or write more than that. You've earned it.

Made in the USA
Columbia, SC
23 January 2020